챗GPT가 골라주는

영어명언 125

필기체로 따라쓰기

챗GPT가 골라주는
영어명언 125
필기체로 따라쓰기

Life is like a box of chocolates.
You never know what you are gonna get.

도서 큰※
출판 그림

아주 오랜 세월 선조들은 자신들의 삶을 통해 얻은 지혜를 명언으로 남겼습니다. 여전히 우리의 삶 속에서 그 명언들은 우리가 자신에게 직면한 문제들을 해결하는 데 유효하며, 지혜를 배우고 교훈을 얻습니다.

챗GPT가 골라주는 명언들은 성공하는 인생, 행복한 삶을 꿈꾸는 사람들에게도 힘을 주지만 현재 힘들고 지친 사람, 잠시 넘어져 정신없는 사람에게도 주변을 둘러보며 천천히 가도 된다고 알려 주는 긍정적인 메시지를 전달하고 있습니다.

영어명언 125의 문장들을 필기체(Parisienne font)로 필사하면서 필기체 마스터가 되어 보세요. 익숙한 영문 고딕체를 보다가 갑자기 필기체를 보면 읽는 것부터 부담스러울 수 있는데 필기체 연습을 해 놓으면 훨씬 자연스럽게 느껴질 것입니다.

영어 문장을 베껴 적다 보면, 여러 가지 도움되는 부분이 많습니다. 영어 문장 독해에 재미가 생깁니다. 짧은 명언을 통째로 외워 활용해 보면, 자존감이 높아집니다. 복잡한 문장은 구와 절로 옮겨 적으면서 문장의 구조를 익혀 보세요. 영작에 도전할 때 많은 도움을 줍니다. 또 영어를 멋있고 개성 있고 세련되게 쓸 수 있습니다. 영어 필기체 모양에 익숙해져 필기체 문장을 읽을 때 막힘이 없습니다.

이렇듯 필기체를 따라 쓰면 독해는 물론 어휘력 향상, 영어 문장 구조 파악, 성취감과 집중력 향상에 큰 도움이 됩니다.

영어명언 125를 필사하기 전에 내가 좋아하는 펜을 미리 준비해 주세요. 참고로 일반적인 볼펜은 쓰다 보면 미끄러지는 느낌과 끈적이는 덩어리가 나오는 단점이 있으니 잘 선택해 주세요.

추천하는 펜으로는 수성펜과 젤펜 그리고 라이너펜과 세필 만년필 등이 있습니다.

수성펜은 점도가 없어 약간 번지는 단점이 있지만 부드럽게 잘 써지고 약간의 힘 조절로 굵기의 변화도 가능합니다.

젤펜(중성펜)은 점도가 볼펜보다는 낮고 수성펜보다는 높은 중간 정도를 가진 펜으로 적당히 부드러운 느낌이 있습니다. 굵기가 다양하니 될 수 있으면 약간 얇은 펜을 추천합니다.

드로잉할 때 친숙한 라이너펜도 글씨 필사할 때 써지는 느낌이 부드럽고 번짐이 없습니다. 마음에 드는 문장 위에 형광펜으로 색을 입혀도 번짐 걱정이 없는 펜입니다.

빠른 시간에 빨리 마스터하려고 하지 말고 하루에 10분씩 매일 한 문장씩 쓰고 많이 읽어 주세요. 명언에서 삶의 지혜를 얻고, 이를 알고 활용함으로써, 대화에서 깊이 있는 논의를 이끌어내고, 상대편에게 긍정적인 인상을 남길 수 있습니다.

큰그림 편집부

Capital letter

$\mathscr{A}$

$\mathscr{B}$

Small letter

a

필기체로
대문자와 소문자를
연습합니다.

가볍게 영어 단어와
짧은 문장으로 필기체
연습을 합니다.

Spring 봄

Spring

Summer 여름

Summer

...nk you for your love 당신...

Thank you for your l...

마음으로 봐야만 제대로 볼 수 있어요.
정말 중요한 것은 눈에 보이지 않아요.

...is only with the heart that one can see rightly;
what is essential is invisible to the eye.

→ 영어명언 한글 해석

→ 영어명언 125

It is only with the heart that one can see

rightly; what is essential is invisible to the ey...

→ 필기체(Parisienne font)
→ 필기체로 따라 써 보세요.
→ 한 번 더 써 보세요.

앙투안 드 생텍쥐페리

→ 명언을 말한 사람

CONTENTS

Cursive handwriting practice

필기체 연습

Capital letter

A   A

B   B

C   C

D   D

E   E

F   F

G   G

H   H

I   I

J   J

K   K

L   L

M   M

N   N

O O

P P

Q Q

R R

S S

T T

U U

V V

W W

X X

Y Y

Z Z

Small letter

a a a   h h h

b b b   i i i

c c c   j j j

d d d   k k k

e e e   l l l

f f f   m m m

g g g   n n n

필기체 소문자

o *o* *o*	*v* *v* *v*
p *p* *p*	*w* *w* *w*
q *q* *q*	*x* *x* *x*
r *r* *r*	*y* *y* *y*
s *s* *s*	*z* *z* *z*
t *t* *t*	
u *u* *u*	

: 단어 써 보기 :

Spring 봄

Spring   *Spring*

Summer 여름

Summer   *Summer*

Fall 가을

Fall   *Fall*

Winter 겨울

Winter   *Winter*

Monday 월요일

Monday *Monday*

Tuesday 화요일

Tuesday *Tuesday*

Wednesday 수요일

Wednesday *Wednesday*

Thursday 목요일

Thursday *Thursday*

Friday 금요일

Friday *Friday*

Saturday 토요일

Saturday *Saturday*

Sunday 일요일

Sunday *Sunday*

 : 짧은 문장 써 보기 :

Happy Birthday 생일 축하합니다.

Happy Birthday

Happy Birthday

Merry Christmas 메리 크리스마스

Merry Christmas

Merry Christmas

Thank you for your love 당신의 사랑에 감사드립니다.

Thank you for your love

Thank you for your love

Children's Day 어린이날

Children's Day

Children's Day

Happy New Year 새해 복 많이 받으세요.

Happy New Year

Happy New Year

You will always have me. 내가 항상 네 옆에 있을 거야.

You will always have me.

You will always have me.

Growing up means adapting. 성장한다는 것은 적응한다는 뜻이지.

Growing up means adapting.

Growing up means adapting.

That was practically my mantra. 그게 사실상 내 좌우명이었어.

That was practically my mantra.

That was practically my mantra.

Nothing is too wonderful to be true.
있지 못할 만큼 너무 근사한 건 없어.(뭐든지 있을 수 있어.)

Nothing is too wonderful to be true.

Nothing is too wonderful to be true.

We are doers not dreamers. 우리는 몽상가가 아니라 행동하는 사람입니다.

We are doers not dreamers.

We are doers not dreamers.

Today decides tomorrow. 오늘이 내일을 결정한다.

Today decides tomorrow.

Today decides tomorrow.

당신다워지세요.

Be yourself.

Be yourself.

아무도 당신에게 잘못하고 있다고 말할 수 없어요.

No one can say you're doing it wrong.

No one can say you're doing it wrong.

그냥 앉아서 네 말을 들어 줄 누군가 있다는 건 좋은 일이야.

It's nice to have someone that will

It's nice to have someone that will

just sit and listen to you.

just sit and listen to you.

들은 것은 잊어버려요. 본 것은 기억해요. 직접 해 본 것은 이해해요.

I hear and I forget. I see and

I hear and I forget. I see and

I remember. I do and I understand.

I remember. I do and I understand.

당신이 돈을 위해 일하지 않는 때가 옵니다.

You reach a point where you don't

You reach a point where you don't

work for money.

work for money.

Life is ...

삶은 ...

인생은 초콜릿 상자 같아요.
당신이 무엇을 얻게 될지 절대 몰라요.

Life is like a box of chocolates.
You never know what you are gonna get.

Life is like a box of chocolates.

Life is like a box of chocolates.

You never know what you are gonna get.

You never know what you are gonna get.

- 영화 'Forrest Gump' 대사 중에서 -

마음으로 봐야만 제대로 볼 수 있어요.
정말 중요한 것은 눈에 보이지 않아요.

**It is only with the heart that one can see rightly;
what is essential is invisible to the eye.**

It is only with the heart that one can see

It is only with the heart that one can see

rightly; what is essential is invisible to the eye.

rightly; what is essential is invisible to the eye.

사랑은 서로 바라보는 것이 아니라,
같은 방향을 함께 바라보는 것입니다.

**Love does not consist in gazing at each other,
but in looking together in the same direction.**

Love does not consist in gazing at each other,

Love does not consist in gazing at each other,

but in looking together in the same direction.

but in looking together in the same direction.

- 앙투안 드 생텍쥐페리 -

③

당신의 장미가 그토록 소중한 건
당신이 장미에게 쏟아부은 시간 때문입니다.

**It is the time you have wasted for your rose
that makes your rose so important.**

It is the time you have wasted for your rose

It is the time you have wasted for your rose

that makes your rose so important.

that makes your rose so important.

사랑하는 것이 있다면, 놓아 주세요.
만약 당신에게 돌아온다면, 그것은 영원히 당신의 것입니다.
만약 그렇지 않다면, 원래부터 그것은 당신 것이 아니었던 거예요.

If you love something, let it go.
If it comes back to you, it's yours forever.
If it doesn't, then it was never meant to be.

If you love something, let it go.

If you love something, let it go.

If it comes back to you, it's yours forever.

If it comes back to you, it's yours forever.

If it doesn't, then it was never meant to be.

If it doesn't, then it was never meant to be.

28

- 익명 -

당신의 가치를 아는 사람들과 함께하세요.
행복해지기 위해서 많은 사람이 필요하진 않아요.
당신을 있는 그대로 인정해 주는 몇 사람만 있으면 되어요.

Be with people who know your worth.
You don't need a lot of people to be happy.
Just a few who appreciate you for who you are.

Be with people who know your worth.

Be with people who know your worth.

You don't need a lot of people to be happy.

You don't need a lot of people to be happy.

Just a few who appreciate you for who you are.

Just a few who appreciate you for who you are.

어리석은 사람은 멀리서 행복을 찾고,
현명한 사람은 자기 발밑에서 행복을 키웁니다.

**The foolish man seeks happliness in the distance,
the wise grows it under his feet.**

The foolish man seeks happliness in the distance,

the wise grows it under his feet.

- 제임스 오펜하임 -

자녀들에게 줄 수 있는 가장 큰 선물은
책임의 뿌리와 독립의 날개입니다.

**The greatest gifts you can give your children
are the roots of responsibility and the wings
of independence.**

The greatest gifts you can give your children are

The greatest gifts you can give your children are

the roots of responsibility

the roots of responsibility

and the wings of independence.

and the wings of independence.

당신이 가진 것에 고마워하세요.
그렇다면 결국 더욱 많은 것을 갖게 될 거예요.

Be thankful for what you have,
you'll end up having more.

Be thankful for what you have,

Be thankful for what you have,

you'll end up having more.

you'll end up having more.

만약 당신이 갖지 못한 것에 집중한다면,
당신은 결코 충분히 가질 수 없을 것입니다.

**If you concentrate on what you don't have,
you will never, ever have enough.**

If you concentrate on what you don't have,

If you concentrate on what you don't have,

you will never, ever have enough.

you will never, ever have enough.

날짜와 함께 적은 꿈은 목표가 됩니다.
목표를 잘게 나누면 계획이 됩니다.
계획을 실행에 옮기면 꿈이 실현됩니다.

A dream written down with a date becomes a Goal.
A goal broken down becomes a Plan.
A plan backed by Action makes your dream come true.

- 오프라 윈프리 -

A dream written down with a date

A dream written down with a date

becomes a Goal.

becomes a Goal.

A goal broken down becomes a Plan.

A goal broken down becomes a Plan.

A plan backed by Action

A plan backed by Action

makes your dream come true.

makes your dream come true.

자신의 삶을 더 많이 칭찬하고 축하할수록,
인생에 축하할 일이 더 많아집니다.

**The more you praise and celebrate your life,
the more there is in life to celebrate.**

The more you praise and celebrate your life,

the more there is in life to celebrate.

- 오프라 윈프리 -

당신이 할 수 있는 가장 큰 모험은
자기가 꿈꾸는 삶을 사는 것입니다.

The biggest adventure you can ever take
is to live the life of your dreams.

The biggest adventure you can ever take

is to live the life of your dreams.

미숙한 사랑은 당신이 필요해서 당신을 사랑한다고 합니다.
성숙한 사랑은 당신을 사랑하니까 당신이 필요하다고 합니다.

Immature love says, I love you because I need you.
Mature love says, I need you because I love you.

- 윈스턴 처칠 -

Immature love says,

Immature love says,

I love you because I need you.

I love you because I need you.

Mature love says,

Mature love says,

I need you because I love you.

I need you because I love you.

비관론자는 모든 기회에서 어려움을 보고,
낙관론자는 모든 어려움에서 기회를 봅니다.

A pessimist sees the difficulty in every opportunity;
an optimist sees the opportunity in every difficulty.

A pessimist sees the difficulty in every

opportunity;

an optimist sees the opportunity in every

difficulty.

- 윈스턴 처칠 - 14

용기란 일어서서 말할 때뿐만 아니라
앉아서 들을 때도 필요한 것입니다.

Courage is what it takes to stand up and speak.
Courage is also what it takes to sit down and listen.

Courage is what it takes to stand up and

Courage is what it takes to stand up and

speak.

speak.

Courage is also what it takes to sit down

Courage is also what it takes to sit down

and listen

and listen

인생을 살아가는 데는 오직 두 가지 방식이 있습니다.
하나는 기적 같은 것은 없다고 믿는 것입니다.
다른 하나는 모든 일이 기적이라고 믿는 것입니다.

There are only two ways to live your life.
One is as though nothing is a miracle.
The other is as though everything is a miracle.

- 알버트 아인슈타인 -

There are only two ways to live your life.

There are only two ways to live your life.

One is as though nothing is a miracle.

One is as though nothing is a miracle.

The other is as though everything is a

The other is as though everything is a

miracle.

miracle.

내 발길을 안내해 주는 램프를 하나만 갖고 있는데
그것은 경험의 램프입니다.
나는 과거 말고는 미래를 판단할 방법을 모릅니다.

I have but one lamp by which my feet are guided
and that is the lamp of experience.
I know no way of judging of the future but by the past.

- 알버트 아인슈타인 -

I have but one lamp by which my feet are

guided and that is the lamp of experience.

I know no way of judging of the future

but by the past.

45

어제로부터 배우고, 오늘을 살아가며,
내일을 희망하세요.

Learn from yesterday, live for today,
hope for tomorrow.

Learn from yesterday, live for today,

hope for tomorrow.

- 알버트 아인슈타인 - ⑱

내일 죽을 것처럼 사세요.
영원히 살 것처럼 배우세요.

Live as if you were to die tomorrow.
Learn as if you were to live forever.

Live as if you were to die tomorrow.

Live as if you were to die tomorrow.

Learn as if you were to live forever.

Learn as if you were to live forever.

만약 우리가 이 세상에서 진정한 평화를 가르치려면,
또한 우리가 전쟁에 맞서 올바른 전쟁을 계속하려면,
우리는 아이들부터 시작해야 할 것입니다.

If we are to teach real peace in this world,
and if we are to carry on a real war against war,
we shall have to begin with the children.

- 마하트마 간디 -

If we are to teach real peace in this world,

If we are to teach real peace in this world,

and if we are to carry on

and if we are to carry on

a real war against war,

a real war against war,

we shall have to begin with the children.

we shall have to begin with the children.

많은 사람들은 무엇이 진정한 행복을 이루는지에 대해
잘못 생각하고 있어요.
행복은 자기 만족이 아니라,
가치 있는 목적을 충실히 해 나가는 것에서 얻을 수 있어요.

Many persons have a wrong idea of what
constitutes true happiness.
It is not attained through self-gratification
but through fidelity to a worthy purpose.

- 헬렌 켈러 - 21

Many persons have a wrong idea of what

Many persons have a wrong idea of what

constitutes true happiness.

constitutes true happiness.

It is not attained through self-gratification

It is not attained through self-gratification

but through fidelity to a worthy purpose.

but through fidelity to a worthy purpose.

당신이 당신을 믿는 남은 유일한 사람일지도 모르지만,
그것으로 충분해요.
어둠의 우주를 뚫는 데는 단 하나의 별이면 됩니다.
절대 포기하지 마세요.

You may be the only person left who believes in you,
but it's enough.
It takes just one star to pierce a universe of darkness.
Never give up.

- 리첼 E. 굿리치 -

You may be the only person left who believes

You may be the only person left who believes

in you, but it's enough.

in you, but it's enough.

It takes just one star to pierce a universe of

It takes just one star to pierce a universe of

darkness. Never give up.

darkness. Never give up.

우리는 장미 덤불에 가시가 있어서 불평할 수도 있고,
또는 가시 덤불에 장미가 있어서 기뻐할 수도 있습니다.

**We can complain because rose bushes have thorns,
or rejoice because thorn bushes have roses.**

We can complain because rose bushes

have thorns, or rejoice because thorn

bushes have roses.

- 아브라함 링컨 -

행복한 결혼 생활을 만드는 데 중요한 것은
당신이 얼마나 잘 어울리느냐가 아니라
당신이 서로 안 맞는 상황에 어떻게 대처하느냐입니다.

**What counts in making a happy marriage
is not so much how compatible you are,
but how you deal with incompatibility.**

What counts in making a happy marriage

is not so much how compatible you are,

but how you deal with incompatibility.

- 레브 톨스토이 -

사랑은 최고의 투자라고들 하죠.
당신이 더 많이 줄수록,
당신에게 더 많은 대가가 돌아옵니다.

**They say love is the best investment;
the more you give,
the more you get in return.**

They say love is the best investment;

the more you give,

the more you get in return.

- 오드리 헵번 -

여러분은 나이가 들면서,
손이 두 개라는 걸 알게 될 겁니다.
한 손은 자신을 돕기 위한 것이고, 또 한 손은 남을 돕기 위한 것입니다.

**As you grow older,
you will discover that you have two hands,
one for helping yourself, the other for helping others.**

As you grow older, you will discover that

As you grow older, you will discover that

you have two hands, one for helping yourself,

you have two hands, one for helping yourself,

the other for helping others.

the other for helping others.

A

우리 모두는 매일 삶을 함께 시간 여행하고 있어요.
우리가 할 수 있는 것은 이 놀라운 여정을 최선을 다해
즐기는 것뿐입니다.

We are all travelling through time together,
everyday of our lives.
All we can do is do our best to relish this
remarkable ride.

- 영화 'About Time' 대사 중에서 -

We are all travelling through time

together, everyday of our lives.

All we can do is do our best to relish

this remarkable ride.

어려움에 웃는 법을 배우지 않으면,
나이가 들었을 때 웃을 일이 전혀 없을 것입니다.

**If you don't learn to laugh at trouble,
you won't have anything to laugh at when you're old.**

If you don't learn to laugh at trouble, you won't

have anything to laugh at when you're old.

- 에드가 왓슨 하우 -

인생에서 가장 큰 영광은 결코 넘어지지 않는 것이 아니라,
넘어질 때마다 다시 일어서는 데 있습니다.

**The greatest glory in living lies not in never falling,
but in rising every time we fall.**

The greatest glory in living lies not in never

falling, but in rising every time we fall.

오늘 누군가가 그늘에 앉아 있을 수 있는 것은
오래전에 누군가가 나무를 심었기 때문입니다.

**Someone's sitting in the shade today
because someone planted a tree a long time ago.**

Someone's sitting in the shade today

Someone's sitting in the shade today

because someone planted a tree a long time ago.

because someone planted a tree a long time ago.

- 워런 버핏 -

걱정은 흔들의자와 같아요. 당신에게 할 무언가를 주지만,
아무데도 데려가지 않습니다. (결국 제자리에 있게 합니다.)

**Worry is like a rocking chair. – it gives you something to do
but it doesn't get you anywhere.**

Worry is like a rocking chair. – it gives you

something to do but it doesn't get you anywhere.

당신의 모든 언행을 칭찬하는 충실한 사람이 아니라,
결점을 친절하게 가르쳐 주는 사람과 가까이하세요.

Think not those faithful who praise all your words and actions, but those who kindly reprove your faults.

Think not those faithful who praise all your

words and actions, but those who kindly reprove

your faults.

-소크라테스-

사람은 소설과 같아요.
맨 마지막 페이지까지 어떻게 끝날지 알 수 없어요.
그렇지 않다면 그것은 읽을 가치가 없을 테니까요.

A man is like a novel;
until the very last page you don't know how it will end.
Otherwise it wouldn't be worth reading.

A man is like a novel; until the very last page

A man is like a novel; until the very last page

you don't know how it will end.

you don't know how it will end.

Otherwise it wouldn't be worth reading.

Otherwise it wouldn't be worth reading.

- 예브게니 자마틴 -

지식을 얻으려면 공부를 해야 하지만,
지혜를 얻으려면 관찰을 해야 합니다.

To acquire knowledge, one must study;
but to acquire wisdom, one must observe.

To acquire knowledge, one must study;

but to acquire wisdom, one must observe.

- 마릴린 보스 사반트 -

배우기만 하고 생각하지 않으면 길을 잃습니다!
생각만 하고 배우지 않으면 위태로워집니다.

He who learns but does not think, is lost!
He who thinks but does not learn is in great danger.

He who learns but does not think, is lost!

He who learns but does not think, is lost!

He who thinks but does not learn is in great

He who thinks but does not learn is in great

danger.

danger.

인생은 롤러코스터와도 같이 오르락내리락하지요.
하지만 소리를 지르든 그것을 즐기든 그건 여러분의 선택입니다.

Life is like a roller coaster. It has its ups and downs.
But it is your choice to scream or enjoy the ride.

Life is like a roller coaster.

Life is like a roller coaster.

It has its ups and downs.

It has its ups and downs.

But it is your choice to scream or enjoy the ride.

But it is your choice to scream or enjoy the ride.

- 익명 -

인생은 우연히 좋아지지 않고,
변화를 통해 나아집니다.

**Your life doesn't get better by chance,
it gets better by change.**

Your life doesn't get better by chance,

it gets better by change.

- 짐 론 -

The most important thing in life is to live in this moment.

살면서 가장 중요한 것은 지금 이 순간을 살아가는 것입니다.

등 뒤로 부는 바람, 앞을 비추는 태양,
당신 옆에 있는 친구들보다 더 좋은 것은 없어요.

**Nothing's better than the wind to your back,
the sun in front of you, and your friends beside you.**

Nothing's better than the wind to your back,

the sun in front of you,

and your friends beside you.

- 애런 더글러스 트림블 -

좋은 친구는 당신의 가장 중요한 인생사를 다 알고,
최고의 친구는 그 일들을 당신과 함께 겪습니다.

**A good friend knows all your best stories,
a best friend has lived them with you.**

A good friend knows all your best stories,

a best friend has lived them with you.

용기란 항상 큰 소리를 내는 것은 아니에요.
때로는 하루가 끝날 때 조용한 목소리로
'내일 다시 해 보겠어.'라고 속삭이는 게 용기일 때도 있어요.

Courage doesen't always roar.
Sometimes it's the quiet voice at the end of the day whispering 'I will try again tomorrow.'

Courage doesen't always roar.

Courage doesen't always roar.

Sometimes it's the quiet voice at the end of the

Sometimes it's the quiet voice at the end of the

day whispering 'I will try again tomorrow.'

day whispering 'I will try again tomorrow.'

74

- 마리 앤 라드마커 -

40

발견이란 진정한 항해는
새로운 풍경을 찾는 것이 아니라,
새로운 눈을 갖는 것에 있습니다.

The real voyage of discovering consists
not in seeking new landscapes,
but in having new eyes.

The real voyage of discovering consists

The real voyage of discovering consists

not in seeking new landscapes,

not in seeking new landscapes,

but in having new eyes.

but in having new eyes.

- 마르셀 프루스트 -

만약 누군가 나를 한 번 배신한다면, 그것은 그 사람의 잘못입니다.
그가 두 번 배신한다면, 그것은 나의 어리석음입니다.

If someone betrays me once, it is his fault;
If he betrays me twice, it is my stupidity.

If someone betrays me once, it is his fault;

If someone betrays me once, it is his fault;

If he betrays me twice, it is my stupidity.

If he betrays me twice, it is my stupidity.

- 엘리너 루스벨트 -

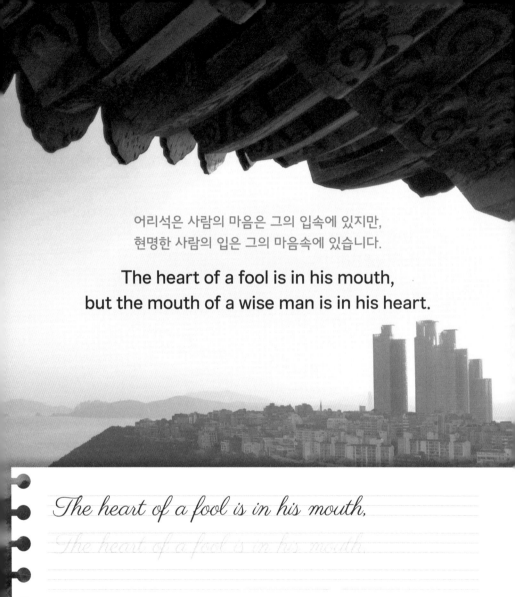

어리석은 사람의 마음은 그의 입속에 있지만,
현명한 사람의 입은 그의 마음속에 있습니다.

**The heart of a fool is in his mouth,
but the mouth of a wise man is in his heart.**

The heart of a fool is in his mouth,

but the mouth of a wise man is in his heart.

- 벤자민 프랭클린 -

역경은 우리가 아직 적응하지 못한 변화일 뿐입니다.
역경은 우리의 삶을 다시 시작하기 위해서 피해야 할 장애물이 아닙니다.
그것은 우리 삶의 일부입니다.

Adversity is just change that we haven't adapted
ourselves to yet.
Adversity isn't an obstacle we need to get around
in order to resume living our life.
It's part of our life.

- 에이미 멀린스 -

Adversity is just change that we haven't

Adversity is just change that we haven't

adapted ourselves to yet. Adversity isn't an

adapted ourselves to yet. Adversity isn't an

obstacle we need to get around in order to

obstacle we need to get around in order to

resume living our life. It's part of our life.

resume living our life. It's part of our life.

많은 인생의 실패자들은 그들이 포기했을 때
성공에 얼마나 가까웠는지 깨닫지 못한 사람들입니다.

Many of life's failures are people who did not realize
how close they were to success when they gave up.

Many of life's failures are people

who did not realize how close

they were to success when they gave up.

- 토마스 에디슨 -

일할 수 있는 특권은 선물입니다.
일할 수 있는 힘은 축복입니다.
일에 대한 사랑은 성공입니다!

**The privilege to work is a gift,
the power to work is a blessing,
the love of work is success!**

The privilege to work is a gift,

the power to work is a blessing,

the love of work is success!

- 데이비드 O. 맥케이 -

강은 알고 있어요.
서두르지 않아도 언젠가는 그곳에 도착하리라는 것을.

**Rivers know this; There is no hurry.
We shall get there some day.**

Rivers know this; There is no hurry.

We shall get there some day.

R

- 만화 영화 '곰돌이 Pooh' 대사 중에서 -
(47)

인생은 자신을 찾는 것이 아닙니다.
인생은 자신을 창조하는 것입니다.

Life isn't about finding yourself.
Life is about creating yourself.

Life isn't about finding yourself.

Life isn't about finding yourself.

Life is about creating yourself.

Life is about creating yourself.

L

자신을 믿어요!
자신의 능력을 신뢰하세요!
자기 자신의 힘에 겸손하지만 합리적인 자신감을 갖지 않으면
성공하거나 행복할 수 없어요.

Believe in yourself!
Have faith in your abilities!
Without a humble but reasonable confidence
in your own powers you cannot be successful
or happy.

- 노먼 빈센트 필 -

Believe in yourself!

Have faith in your abilities!

Without a humble but reasonable

confidence in your own powers

you cannot be successful or happy.

꿈을 따라가다 보면,
꿈꾸는 대로 살고자 노력한다면,
그 꿈은 의외로 일상이 될 것입니다.

If you follow your dream,
if you try to live as you dream,
the dream will be everyday life unexpectedly.

If you follow your dream,

if you try to live as you dream,

the dream will be everyday life unexpectedly.

- 헨리 데이비드 소로 -

당신이 할 수 있는 것이든
꿈을 꿀 수 있는 무엇이든, 시작하세요.
대담함 속에 천재성과 힘, 그리고 마법이 있습니다.

**Whatever you can do or dream you can,
begin it.
Boldness has genius, power and magic in it.**

Whatever you can do or dream you can,

Whatever you can do or dream you can,

begin it.

begin it.

Boldness has genius, power and magic in it.

Boldness has genius, power and magic in it.

웃음은 가장 값싸고
가장 효과적인 경이로운 약입니다.
웃음은 만병통치약입니다.

Laughter is the most inexpensive
& most effective wonder drug.
Laughter is a universal medicine.

Laughter is the most inexpensive

& most effective wonder drug.

Laughter is a universal medicine.

- 버트런드 러셀 -

젊음은 아름다움을 보는 능력이 있기 때문에 행복합니다.
아름다움을 볼 수 있는 능력을 간직하는 사람은
결코 늙지 않습니다.

Youth is happy because it has the ability
to see beauty. Anyone who keeps the ability
to see beauty never grows old.

Youth is happy because it has the ability

Youth is happy because it has the ability

to see beauty. Anyone who keeps the ability

to see beauty. Anyone who keeps the ability

to see beauty never grows old.

to see beauty never grows old.

감사의 마음을 갖는다면 평범한 날을 명절같이,
일상적인 일들을 즐거움으로,
평범한 기회를 축복처럼 느낄 것입니다.

Gratitude can transform common days
into thanksgiving, turn routine jobs into joy,
and change ordinary opportunities
into blessings.

- 윌리엄 아서 워드

54

Gratitude can transform common days into

Gratitude can transform common days into

thanksgiving, turn routine jobs into joy,

thanksgiving, turn routine jobs into joy,

and change ordinary opportunities into

and change ordinary opportunities into

blessings.

blessings.

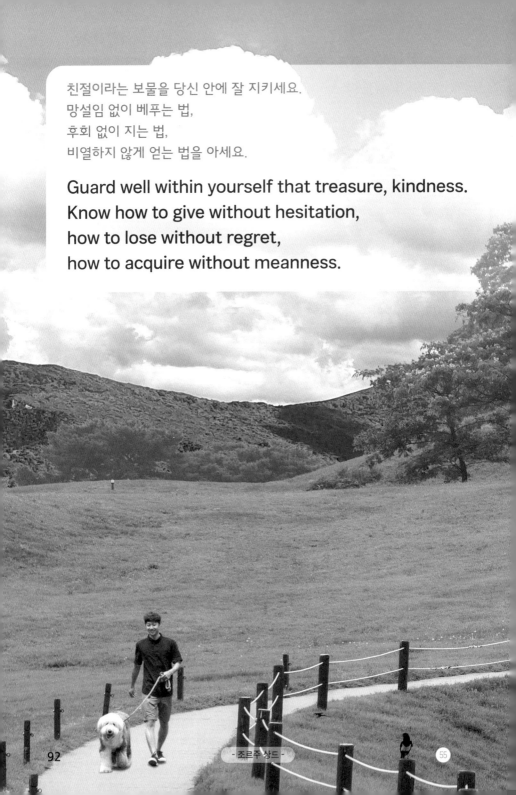

친절이라는 보물을 당신 안에 잘 지키세요.
망설임 없이 베푸는 법,
후회 없이 지는 법,
비열하지 않게 얻는 법을 아세요.

Guard well within yourself that treasure, kindness.
Know how to give without hesitation,
how to lose without regret,
how to acquire without meanness.

- 조르주 상드 -

Guard well within yourself that treasure,

Guard well within yourself that treasure,

kindness.

kindness.

Know how to give without hesitation,

Know how to give without hesitation,

how to lose without regret,

how to lose without regret,

how to acquire without meanness.

how to acquire without meanness.

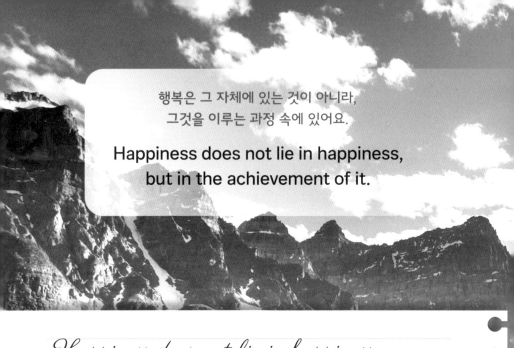

행복은 그 자체에 있는 것이 아니라,
그것을 이루는 과정 속에 있어요.

**Happiness does not lie in happiness,
but in the achievement of it.**

Happiness does not lie in happiness,

Happiness does not lie in happiness,

but in the achievement of it.

but in the achievement of it.

ℋ

- 표도르 도스토예프스키 -

행복은 당신이 경험하는 것이 아니라,
기억하는 것입니다.

**Happiness isn't something you experience;
It's something you remember.**

Happiness isn't something you experience;

Happiness isn't something you experience;

It's something you remember.

It's something you remember.

인간의 감정은 만나고 이별할 때
가장 순수하며 가장 빛이 납니다.

Man's feelings are always purest and most glowing in the hour of meeting and of farewell.

Man's feelings are always purest and most

glowing in the hour of meeting and of farewell.

장 폴 리히터

공감이란 다른 사람들이 경험하고 있는 것에 대하여
존중하는 마음으로 이해하는 것입니다.

Empathy is a respectful understanding
of what others are experiencing.

Empathy is a respectful understanding

of what others are experiencing.

- 마셜 로젠버그 -

만약 우리 모두가 할 수 있는 일을 해낸다면,
우리 자신이 그야말로 놀라게 될 것입니다.

If we all did the things
we are capable of doing,
we would literally astound ourselves.

If we all did the things we are capable of

doing, we would literally astound ourselves.

98

- 토마스 에디슨 -

(60)

성공한 사람보다는
가치 있는 사람이 되려고 노력하세요.

**Try not to become a man of success
but rather try to become a man of value.**

Try not to become a man of success

Try not to become a man of success

but rather try to become a man of value.

but rather try to become a man of value.

사람에 대한 최고의 척도는
안락하고 편리한 순간에 보여 주는 모습이 아니라,
도전과 논란의 시기에 보여 주는 모습입니다.

The ultimate measure of a person is not
where they stand in moments of comfort and
convenience, but where they stand in times of
challenge and controversy.

- 마틴 루터 킹 주니어 -

The ultimate measure of a person is not

The ultimate measure of a person is not

where they stand in moments of comfort

where they stand in moments of comfort

and convenience, but where they stand

and convenience, but where they stand

in times of challenge and controversy.

in times of challenge and controversy.

자신을 다룰 땐, 머리를 사용하세요.
다른 사람들을 다룰 땐, 마음을 사용하세요.

To handle yourself, use your head.
To handle others, use your heart.

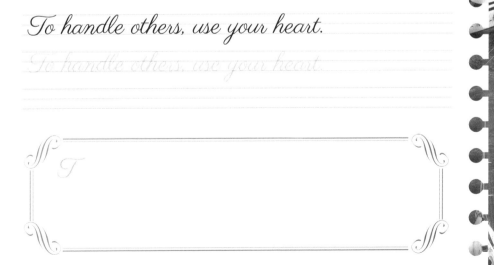

To handle yourself, use your head.

To handle others, use your heart.

- 엘리너 루스벨트 -

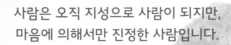

사람은 오직 지성으로 사람이 되지만,
마음에 의해서만 진정한 사람입니다.

**Man becomes man only by his intelligence,
but he is man only by his heart.**

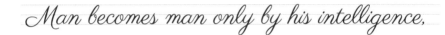

Man becomes man only by his intelligence,

Man becomes man only by his intelligence,

but he is man only by his heart.

but he is man only by his heart.

M

- 앙리 F. 아미엘 -

인생에서 가장 큰 즐거움은
사람들이 당신은 할 수 없을 거라 말한 것을 해내는 것입니다.

**The greatest pleasure in life is doing
what people say you cannot do.**

The greatest pleasure in life is doing

what people say you cannot do.

- 월터 베이지호트 -

이 세상에 당신은 한 사람일지도 모르지만,
어떤 한 사람에게 당신은 세상의 전부일 수도 있습니다.

To the world you may be one person,
but to one person you may be the world.

To the world you may be one person,

but to one person you may be the world.

- 브랜디 스나이더 -

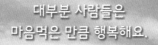

대부분 사람들은
마음먹은 만큼 행복해요.

**Most folks are about as happy
as they make up their minds to be.**

Most folks are about as happy as they make

up their minds to be.

106   - 아브라함 링컨 -   (67)

아름다운 젊은이는 우연한 자연현상이지만,
아름다운 노인은 예술작품입니다.

Beautiful young people are accidents of nature,
but beautiful old people are works of art.

Beautiful young people are accidents of nature,

but beautiful old people are works of art.

재능은 고독 속에서 가장 잘 길러집니다.
그러나 인격은 세상의 험난한 풍파 속에서 가장 잘 형성됩니다.

Talents are best nurtured in solitude;
but character is best formed
in the stormy billows of the world.

Talents are best nurtured in solitude;

but character is best formed in the stormy

billows of the world.

108 · 요한 존 헨리 폰 괴테 · 69

다른 사람이 하는 일에 신경 쓰지 마세요.
자신보다 더 잘하고, 하루하루 자신의 기록을 깨면,
당신은 성공한 사람입니다.

Never mind what others do;
do better than yourself, beat your own record
from day to day, and you are a success.

Never mind what others do;

Never mind what others do;

do better than yourself, beat your own record

do better than yourself, beat your own record

from day to day, and you are a success.

from day to day, and you are a success.

- 윌리엄 존 헨리 보에커 -

우리는 사람들을 그들이 오른 최고의 경지로 판단해서는 안 됩니다.
그들이 출발한 지점부터 거쳐 온 거리로 평가해야 합니다.

We should not judge people
by their peak of excellence;
but by the distance they have traveled
from the point where they started.

- 헨리 비처 -

We should not judge people

We should not judge people

by their peak of excellence;

by their peak of excellence;

but by the distance they have traveled

but by the distance they have traveled

from the point where they started.

from the point where they started.

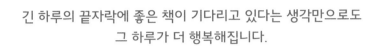

긴 하루의 끝자락에 좋은 책이 기다리고 있다는 생각만으로도
그 하루가 더 행복해집니다.

Just the knowledge that a good book
is awaiting one at the end of a long day
makes that day happier.

Just the knowledge that a good book

is awaiting one at the end of a long day

makes that day happier.

- 캐슬린 노리스 -

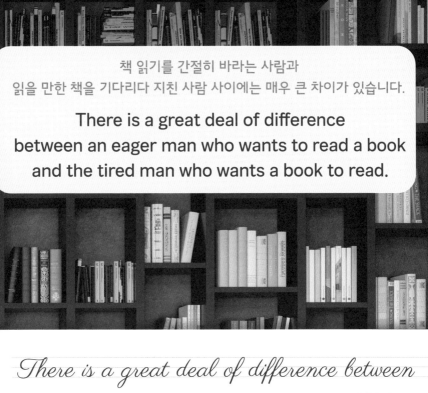

책 읽기를 간절히 바라는 사람과
읽을 만한 책을 기다리다 지친 사람 사이에는 매우 큰 차이가 있습니다.

**There is a great deal of difference
between an eager man who wants to read a book
and the tired man who wants a book to read.**

There is a great deal of difference between

There is a great deal of difference between

an eager man who wants to read a book and

an eager man who wants to read a book and

the tired man who wants a book to read.

the tired man who wants a book to read.

인생이 그대를 힘든 상황에 처하게 할 때면,
"왜 나야?"라고 말하지 말고, 그냥 "해봐라."라고 말해 보세요.

**When life puts you in tough situations,
don't say "why me?" just say "try me."**

When life puts you in tough situations,

don't say "why me?" just say "try me."

- 익명 -

삶은 항상 당신에게 두 번째의 기회를 줍니다.
그것은 '내일'이라고 합니다.

**Life always offers you
a second chance.
It's called "Tomorrow".**

Life always offers you a second chance.

Life always offers you a second chance.

It's called "Tomorrow".

It's called "Tomorrow".

L

그대가 자존감을 지키고자 한다면
그릇되다고 알고 있는 일을 함으로써 잠시 사람들을 기분 좋게 하는 것보다,
옳다고 알고 있는 일을 함으로써 사람들을 불쾌하게 하는 것이 낫다.

That you may retain your self-respect,
it is better to displease the people
by doing what you know is right,
than to temporarily please them
by doing what you know is wrong.

116   - 윌리엄 존 헨리 보에커 -   ⁷⁶

That you may retain your self-respect,

That you may retain your self-respect,

it is better to displease the people

it is better to displease the people

by doing what you know is right,

by doing what you know is right,

than to temporarily please them

than to temporarily please them

by doing what you know is wrong.

by doing what you know is wrong.

우리의 모든 꿈은 이루어질 수 있어요.
우리가 꿈을 좇을 용기만 있다면.

**All our dreams can come true,
if we have the courage to pursue them.**

All our dreams can come true,

All our dreams can come true,

if we have the courage to pursue them.

if we have the courage to pursue them.

A

- 월트 디즈니 -

꿈은 이루어집니다. 그럴 가능성이 없다면,
자연은 우리에게 꿈을 꾸게 하지 않았을 것입니다.

**Dreams come true. Without that possibility,
nature would not incite us to have them.**

Dreams come true. Without that possibility,

Dreams come true. Without that possibility,

nature would not incite us to have them.

nature would not incite us to have them.

D

- 존 업다이크 -

좋은 책을 읽는 것은 지난 세기의
가장 훌륭한 사람들과 대화하는 것과 같습니다.

The reading of all good books
is like a conversation
with the finest men of past centuries.

The reading of all good books is like a

The reading of all good books is like a

conversation with the finest men of past

conversation with the finest men of past

centuries.

centuries.

- 르네 데카르트 -

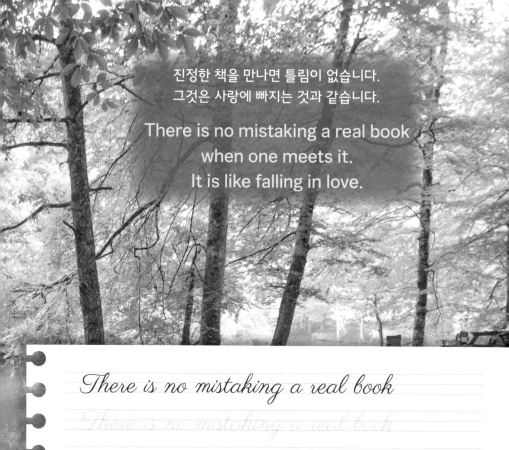

진정한 책을 만나면 틀림이 없습니다.
그것은 사랑에 빠지는 것과 같습니다.

There is no mistaking a real book
when one meets it.
It is like falling in love.

There is no mistaking a real book

when one meets it.

It is like falling in love.

언제나 화를 내거나 불평한다면,
사람들은 당신을 위해 시간을 내지 않을 거예요.

**People won't have time for you
if you are always angry or complaining.**

People won't have time for you

People won't have time for you

if you are always angry or complaining.

if you are always angry or complaining.

P

- 스티븐 호킹 -

가진 것을 다 보여 주지 말고,
아는 것보다 적게 말하세요.

Have more than thou showest,
speak less than thou knowest.

Have more than thou showest,

Have more than thou showest,

speak less than thou knowest.

speak less than thou knowest.

H

- '리어왕' 중에서 -

당신의 이 세 가지 면을 볼 수 있는 사람만 믿으세요.
당신 미소 뒤에 있는 슬픔, 당신의 분노 뒤에 있는 사랑,
당신이 침묵하는 이유.

Only trust someone
who can see these three things in you;
the sorrow behind your smile,
the love behind your anger,
and the reason behind your silence.

- 익명 -

Only trust someone who can see these three

Only trust someone who can see these three

things in you; the sorrow behind your smile,

things in you; the sorrow behind your smile,

the love behind your anger,

the love behind your anger,

and the reason behind your silence.

and the reason behind your silence.

시작도 끝도 없습니다.
단지 삶의 무한한 열정만 있을 뿐입니다.

There is no end. There is no beginning.
There is only the infinite passion of life.

There is no end. There is no beginning.

There is only the infinite passion of life.

- 페데리코 펠리니 -

(84)

존경의 가장 진실된 형태 중 하나는
실제로 상대편이 말하는 것을 들어주는 것입니다.

**One of the most sincere forms of respect is
actually listening to what another has to say.**

One of the most sincere forms of respect is

actually listening to what another has to say.

- 브라이언트 H. 맥길 -

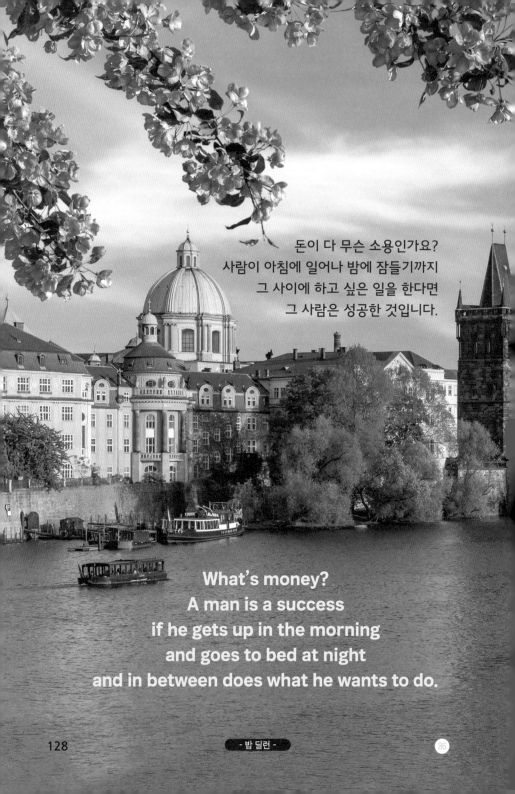

돈이 다 무슨 소용인가요?
사람이 아침에 일어나 밤에 잠들기까지
그 사이에 하고 싶은 일을 한다면
그 사람은 성공한 것입니다.

What's money?
A man is a success
if he gets up in the morning
and goes to bed at night
and in between does what he wants to do.

128
- 밥 딜런 -
86

What's money?

What's money?

A man is a success if he gets up

A man is a success if he gets up

in the morning and goes to bed at night

in the morning and goes to bed at night

and in between does what he wants to do.

and in between does what he wants to do.

빨리 가려면 혼자 가고,
멀리 가려면 함께 가세요.

If you want to go fast, go alone.
If you want to go far, go together.

If you want to go fast, go alone.

If you want to go far, go together.

- 아프리카 속담 -

그것이 만약 옳다면 이루어지게 되어 있어요.
중요한 것은 서두르지 않는 것입니다.
소중한 것은 사라지지 않거든요.

If it is right, it bappens.
The main thing is not to burry.
Nothing good gets away.

If it is right, it bappens.

If it is right, it bappens.

The main thing is not to burry.

The main thing is not to burry.

Nothing good gets away.

Nothing good gets away.

- 존 스타인벡 -

날아갈 수 없으면 뛰고,
달릴 수 없으면 걷고,
걸을 수 없으면 기어가지만,
무슨 일을 하든지 쉬지 말고 앞으로 나아가야 해요.

If you can't fly then run,
if you can't run then walk,
if you can't walk then crawl,
but whatever you do you have to keep
moving forward.

- 마틴 루터 킹 주니어 -

If you can't fly then run,

If you can't fly then run,

if you can't run then walk,

if you can't run then walk,

if you can't walk then crawl,

if you can't walk then crawl,

but whatever you do you have to keep

but whatever you do you have to keep

moving forward.

moving forward.

잘못된 것에 너무 연연하지 마세요.
그 대신 다음에 할 일에 집중하세요.
해답을 향해 함께 나아가는 데 에너지를 소비하세요.

Don't dwell on what went wrong.
Instead, focus on what to do next.
Spend your energy moving forward
together towards an answer.

- 데니스 웨이틀리 -

Don't dwell on what went wrong.

Don't dwell on what went wrong.

Instead, focus on what to do next.

Instead, focus on what to do next.

Spend your energy moving forward

Spend your energy moving forward

together towards an answer.

together towards an answer.

대부분의 사람들이 목표에 도달하지 못하는 이유는
목표를 명확히 정의하지 않거나,
그 목표를 이룰 수 있다고 진지하게 생각하지 않기 때문입니다.
승자들은 자신이 어디로 가고 있는지, 그 길을 가면서 무엇을 할 계획인지,
그 모험을 누구와 함께 할 것인지를 말할 수 있습니다.

The reason most people never reach thier

goals is that they don't define them,

or ever seriously consider them

as believable or achievable.

The reason most people never reach thier goals is that they don't define them, or ever seriously consider them as believable or achievable. Winners can tell you where they are going, what they plan to do along the way, and who will be sharing the adventure with them.

Winners can tell you where they are

going, what they plan to do along the way,

and who will be sharing the adventure

with them.

- 데니스 웨이틀리 -

운명은 우연의 문제가 아닌 선택의 문제입니다.
그것은 기다리는 것이 아니라 성취해 나가는 것입니다.

Destiny is not a matter of chance,
but a matter of choice;
It is not a thing to be waited for,
it is a thing to be achieved.

Destiny is not a matter of chance, but a matter
of choice; It is not a thing to be waited for, it is
a thing to be achieved.

138   - 윌리엄 제닝스 브라이언 -

과거에 머무르지 말고,
미래를 꿈꾸지 말고,
현재의 순간에 마음을 집중하세요.

Do not dwell in the past,
do not dream of the future,
concentrate the mind on the present moment.

Do not dwell in the past, do not dream of the
future, concentrate the mind on the present
moment.

좋아하는 것과 사랑하는 것의 차이는 무엇입니까?
부처님께서 답했습니다.
"꽃을 좋아한다면 꺾기 마련이지만,
꽃을 사랑한다면 매일 물을 준다!"
이 말을 이해한다면, 인생을 이해하는 겁니다.

What is the difference between I like you and I love you?
Beautifully answered by Buddha;
"When you like a flower, you just pluck it.
But when you love a flower, you water it daily!"
One who unerstands this, understands life ...

*What is the difference between I like you and
I love you?
Beautifully answered by Buddha;
"When you like a flower, you just pluck it.
But when you love a flower, you water it daily!"
One who unerstands this, understands life ...*

What is the difference between I like you and
I love you?
Beautifully answered by Buddha:
"When you like a flower, you just pluck it.
But when you love a flower, you water it daily!"
One who understands this, understands life.

평화는 내면에서 비롯됩니다. 외부에서 찾지 마세요.

Peace comes from within. Do not seek it without.

Peace comes from within.

Do not seek it without.

Peace comes from within.

Do not seek it without.

마음이 모든 것입니다. 당신이 생각하는 것이 당신이 됩니다.

The mind is everything. What you think you become.

The mind is everything.

What you think you become.

The mind is everything.

What you think you become.

- 붓다 -

고통의 근원은 집착입니다.

The root of suffering is attachment.

The root of suffering is attachment.

The root of suffering is attachment.

당신 스스로 말고는 다른 누구에게도 안식처를 찾지 마세요.

Do not look for a sanctuary in anyone except yourself.

Do not look for a sanctuary in anyone except yourself.

Do not look for a sanctuary in anyone except yourself.

인생의 목적은 성취가 아니라 경험입니다.

The purpose of life is not achievement, but experience.

The purpose of life is not achievement, but experience.

The purpose of life is not achievement, but experience.

절제된 마음은 행복을 가져다 줍니다.

A disciplined mind brings happiness.

A disciplined mind brings happiness.

A disciplined mind brings happiness.

나 자신을 진실로 알게 되면, 모든 것이 달라집니다.

When you truly know yourself, everything changes.

When you truly know yourself, everything changes.

When you truly know yourself, everything changes.

인생에서 가장 중요한 것은 지금 이 순간을 살아가는 것입니다.

The most important thing in life is to live in this moment.

The most important thing in life is to live in this moment.

The most important thing in life is to live in this moment.

독서하는 습관을 들이는 것은 인생의 거의 모든
불행으로부터 스스로 피난처를 마련하는 것입니다.

**To acquire the habit of reading is
to construct for yourself a refuge
from almost all the miseries of life.**

*To acquire the habit of reading is to construct
for yourself a refuge from almost all the
miseries of life.*

*To acquire the habit of reading is to construct
for yourself a refuge from almost all the
miseries of life.*

146   - 윌리엄 서머셋 몸 -

한 문장이라도 매일 조금씩 읽기로 결심하세요.
하루 15분씩 시간을 내면 연말에는 변화가 느껴질 것입니다.

Resolve to edge in a little reading every day, if it is but a single sentence.
If you gain fifteen minutes a day, it will make itself felt at the end of the year.

Resolve to edge in a little reading every day,
if it is but a single sentence.
If you gain fifteen minutes a day, it will
make itself felt at the end of the year.

Resolve to edge in a little reading every day,
if it is but a single sentence.
If you gain fifteen minutes a day, it will
make itself felt at the end of the year.

미래를 내다보며 점들을 이을 수는 없어요.
과거를 되돌아보면서만 점들을 이을 수 있지요.
그러니까 점들이 어떤 식으로든 미래로 연결될 것을 믿어야 합니다.
당신의 직감, 운명, 삶, 업보 뭐든 간에 믿어야 해요.
이 접근법은 절대 저를 실망시킨 적이 없으며 제 삶에 모든 변화를 가져왔어요.

You can't connect the dots looking forward; you can only connect them looking backwards. So you have to trust that the dots will somehow connect in your future. You have to trust in something? your gut, destiny, life, karma, whatever. This approach has never let me down, and it has made all the difference in my life.

You can't connect the dots looking forward; you can only connect them looking backwards. So you have to trust that the dots will somehow connect in your future. You have to trust in something? your gut, destiny, life, karma, whatever. This approach has never let me down, and it has made all the difference in my life.

- 스티브 잡스 -

You can't connect the dots looking forward; you can only connect them looking backwards. So you have to trust that the dots will somehow connect in your future. You have to trust in something? your gut, destiny, life, karma, whatever. This approach has never let me down, and it has made all the difference in my life.

제가 계속 나아갈 수 있던 유일한 이유는
제가 하는 일을 사랑했기 때문이라 확신합니다.
당신이 사랑하는 것을 찾으셔야 합니다.
그리고 당신이 연인을 찾아야 하듯 일 또한 마찬가지입니다.

I'm convinced that the only thing
that kept me going was that I loved what I did.
You've got to find what you love.
And that is as true for your work
as it is for your lovers.

- 스티브 잡스 -

I'm convinced that the only thing that kept

me going was that I loved what I did.

You've got to find what you love.

And that is as true for your work as it is

for your lovers.

당신의 일은 삶에서 아주 큰 부분을 차지할 것이고, 진정으로 만족할 수 있는 유일한 방법은 당신이 훌륭하다고 믿는 일을 하는 것이죠.
그리고 훌륭한 일을 할 수 있는 유일한 방법은 당신이 좋아하는 일을 하는 겁니다. 아직 찾지 못했다면, 계속 찾아보세요. 안주하지 마세요.
마음의 모든 문제가 그렇듯 발견하면 알 수 있습니다.

Your work is going to fill a large part of your life, and the only way to be truly satisfied is to do what you believe is great work. And the only way to do great work is to love what you do.
If you haven't found it yet, keep looking. Don't settle. As with all matters of the heart, you'll know when you find it.

Your work is going to fill a large part of your life, and the only way to be truly satisfied is to do what you believe is great work. And the only way to do great work is to love what you do. If you haven't found it yet, keep looking. Don't settle. As with all matters of the heart, you'll know when you find it.

- 스티브 잡스 -

Your work is going to fill a large part of your life, and the only way to be truly satisfied is to do what you believe is great work. And the only way to do great work is to love what you do. If you haven't found it yet, keep looking. Don't settle. As with all matters of the heart, you'll know when you find it.

지난 33년 동안 저는 매일 아침 거울을 들여다보며 스스로에게 물었습니다.
오늘이 내 인생의 마지막 날이라면, 난 오늘 하려고 한 일을 하고 싶을까?
그리고 여러 날 동안 계속 '아니'라는 대답이 나올 때마다
저는 무언가를 바꿔야 한다는 것을 알고 있습니다.

For the past 33 years, I have looked in the mirror every morning and asked myself;
'If today were the last day of my life, would I want to do what I am about to do today?'
And whenever the answer has been 'No' for too many days in a row, I know I need to change something.

For the past 33 years, I have looked in the mirror every morning and asked myself;
'If today were the last day of my life, would I want to do what I am about to do today?'
And whenever the answer has been 'No' for too many days in a row, I know I need to change something.

- 스티브 잡스 -

For the past 33 years, I have looked in the mirror every morning and asked myself: "If today were the last day of my life, would I want to do what I am about to do today?" And whenever the answer has been No for too many days in a row, I know I need to change something.

여러분의 시간은 한정되어 있으니,
다른 이의 삶을 살면서 시간을 낭비하지 마세요.
독단적인 견해에 갇히지 마세요.
그것은 다른 사람이 생각한 결과에 따라 살아가는 것이니까요.
다른 사람의 의견 소음이 자기 내면의 목소리를 삼켜 버리지 않도록 하세요.
그리고 무엇보다 가장 중요한 것은
당신의 마음과 직관을 따를 용기를 내는 것입니다.

Your time is limited, so don't waste it living someone else's life. Don't be trapped by dogma — which is living with the results of other people's thinking. Don't let the noise of others' opinions drown out your own inner voice. And most important, have the courage to follow your heart and intuition.

Your time is limited, so don't waste it living someone else's life.
Don't be trapped by dogma — which is living with the results of other people's thinking.
Don't let the noise of others' opinions drown out your own inner voice.
And most important, have the courage to follow your heart and intuition.

- 스티브 잡스 -

Your time is limited, so don't waste it living someone else's life.

Don't be trapped by dogma — which is living with the results of other people's thinking.

Don't let the noise of others' opinions drown out your own inner voice.

And most important, have the courage to follow your heart and intuition.

Life is worth living as long as there's a laugh in it.

웃음이 있는 한, 인생은 살아갈 가치가 있어요.

저에게 글쓰기의 가장 큰 즐거움은 무엇에 관한 것이 아니라
단어들이 만들어 내는 내면의 음악입니다.
그 음악을 포착할 수 있다면
저는 가치 있는 일을 해냈다고 느낍니다.

To me, the greatest pleasure of writing is
not what it's about, but the inner music that
words make. If I can just capture that music,
I feel I've done something worthwhile.

- 트루먼 커포티 -

To me, the greatest pleasure of writing is

To me, the greatest pleasure of writing is

not what it's about,

not what it's about,

but the inner music that words make.

but the inner music that words make.

If I can just capture that music,

If I can just capture that music,

I feel I've done something worthwhile.

I feel I've done something worthwhile.

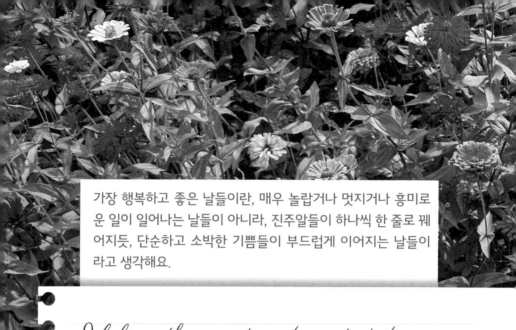

가장 행복하고 좋은 날들이란, 매우 놀랍거나 멋지거나 흥미로운 일이 일어나는 날들이 아니라, 진주알들이 하나씩 한 줄로 꿰어지듯, 단순하고 소박한 기쁨들이 부드럽게 이어지는 날들이라고 생각해요.

I believe the nicest and sweetest days are

not those on which anything very

splendid or wonderful or exciting happens

I believe the nicest and sweetest days are not those on which anything very splendid or wonderful or exciting happens but just those that bring simple little pleasures, following one another softly, like pearls slipping off a string.

but just those that bring simple little

pleasures, following one another softly,

like pearls slipping off a string.

- '빨간 머리 앤' 중에서 -

오, 야망이 있다는 건 즐거워요. 아주 많아서 참 기뻐요.
그리고 야망에는 결코 끝이 없는 것 같아요. 그것이 제일 좋은 점이지요.
한 가지 목표를 이루자마자
더 높은 곳에서 반짝이는 다른 야망을 보게 되지요.
그래서 삶이 매우 재미있는 건가 봐요.

Oh, it's delightful to have ambitions.

I'm so glad I have such a lot.

And there never seems to be any end to

them ... that's the best of it.

Oh, it's delightful to have ambitions. I'm so glad I have such a lot. And there never seems to be any end to them … that's the best of it. Just as soon as you attain to one ambition you see another one glittering higher up still. It does make life so interesting.

Just as soon as you attain to one ambition

you see another one glittering higher up still.

It does make life so interesting.

그녀의 충고는 꼭 후춧가루 같아.
조금만 넣으면 훌륭할 텐데… 그녀는 많이 뿌려서 너무 매워.

**Her advice is much like pepper, I think … execellent in
small quantities but rather scorching in her doses.**

Her advice is much like pepper, I think…

Her advice is much like pepper, I think…

execellent in small quantities

execellent in small quantities

but rather scorching in her doses.

but rather scorching in her doses.

- '에이번리의 앤' 중에서 -

이 세상엔 좋은 게 한 가지가 있어요…
그것은 앞으로도 봄이 계속 온다는 사실이에요.

**That is one good thing about this world…
there are always sure to be more springs.**

That is one good thing about this world…

That is one good thing about this world…

there are always sure to be more springs.

there are always sure to be more springs.

- '에이번리의 앤' 중에서 -

내가 좋아하는 사람이 나를 좋아해 주는 것은
기적입니다.

**It's the miracle
that the person who I like likes me.**

It's the miracle that the person who
I like likes me.

It's the miracle that the person who
I like likes me.

- '어린 왕자' 중에서 -

때때로 작은 일은 다른 날로 미루는 것이
나쁘지 않을 수도 있어요.

**Sometimes, there is no harm in putting off
a piece of work until another day.**

*Sometimes, there is no harm in putting off
a piece of work until another day.*

*Sometimes, there is no harm in putting off
a piece of work until another day.*

사막이 아름다운 건
어딘가에 우물을 숨기고 있기 때문이에요.

**What makes the desert beautiful
is that somewhere it hides a well.**

*What makes the desert beautiful is that
somewhere it hides a well.*

*What makes the desert beautiful is that
somewhere it hides a well.*

- '어린 왕자' 중에서 -

별 중 하나에서 내가 살고 있을 거예요. 그중 하나에서 내가 웃고 있을 거예요.
그래서 밤하늘을 볼 때 마치 모든 별들이 웃고 있는 것처럼 느껴질 거예요.

In one of the stars I shall be living.
In one of them I shall be laughing.
And so it will be as if all the stars were laughing,
when you look at the sky at night.

In one of the stars I shall be living.
In one of them I shall be laughing.
And so it will be as if all the stars were
laughing, when you look at the sky at night.

In one of the stars I shall be living.
In one of them I shall be laughing.
And so it will be as if all the stars were
laughing, when you look at the sky at night.

- '어린 왕자' 중에서 -

"사람들은 어디에 있어?" 마침내 어린 왕자가 말을 이었어요.
"사막에서는 조금 외롭구나…"
"사람들과 함께 있어도 외로워." 뱀이 말했어요.

"Where are the people?"
resumed the little prince at last.
"It's a little lonely in the desert …"
"It is lonely when you're among people, too,"
said the snake.

"Where are the people?"
resumed the little prince at last.
"It's a little lonely in the desert…"
"It is lonely when you're among people, too,"
said the snake.

172

- '어린 왕자' 중에서 -

음, 나비들과 친해지려면
두세 마리의 애벌레들과 있는 걸 견뎌야 해요.

Well, I must endure the presence of two or three caterpillars if I wish to become acquainted with the butterflies.

Well, I must endure the presence of two or three caterpillars if I wish to become acquainted with the butterflies.

만약 당신이 나를 길들인다면, 우리는 서로 필요하게 될 거예요.
나에게 당신은 세상에서 단 하나뿐인 존재가 되고,
당신에게 나는 세상에서 둘도 없는 존재가 될 테니까요.

If you tame me, then we shall need each other.
To me, you will be unique in all the world.
To you, I shall be unique in all the world.

If you tame me, then we shall need each other.
To me, you will be unique in all the world.
To you, I shall be unique in all the world.

If you tame me, then we shall need each other.
To me, you will be unique in all the world.
To you, I shall be unique in all the world.

174   - '어린 왕자' 중에서 -   (121)

사람들은 모두 이미 만들어진 물건들을 가게에서 사지요.
하지만 그 어디에도 우정을 살 수 있는 가게는 없어요.
그래서 사람들은 이제 친구가 하나도 없게 된 거예요.

**They buy things all ready made at the shops.
But there is no shop anywhere where one can buy
friendship, and so men have no friends any more.**

They buy things all ready made at the shops.
But there is no shop anywhere where one
can buy friendship, and so men have no
friends any more.

They buy things all ready made at the shops.
But there is no shop anywhere where one
can buy friendship, and so men have no
friends any more.

- '어린 왕자' 중에서 -

하지만 만약 당신이 나를 길들인다면
마치 내 인생에 태양이 비추는 것과 같을 거예요.
나는 다른 모든 소리와 구분되는 발소리를 알게 될 거예요.
다른 발소리는 나를 땅 밑으로 서둘러 숨게 만들지만,
당신의 발소리는 마치 음악처럼 나를 굴 밖으로 불러낼 것입니다.

But if you tame me, it will be as if the sun came to shine on my life. I shall know the sound of a step that will be different from all the others. Other steps send me hurrying back underneath the ground. Yours will call me, like music, out of my burrow.

But if you tame me, it will be as if the sun came to shine on my life. I shall know the sound of a step that will be different from all the others. Other steps send me hurrying back underneath the ground. Yours will call me, like music, out of my burrow.

176　　　- '어린 왕자' 중에서 -　　(123)

But if you tame me, it will be as if the sun came to shine on my life. I shall know the sound of a step that will be different from all the others. Other steps send me hurrying back underneath the ground. Yours will call me, like music, out of my burrow.

당신은 아름답지만 공허합니다. 아무도 당신을 위해 죽을 수는 없으니까요. 물론 평범한 지나가는 사람에게는 나의 꽃—내 소유의 장미도 당신들과 똑같겠지요.
그렇지만 그 꽃 한 송이가 당신들 다른 수백 송이 장미 모두를 합친 것보다 소중해요. 내가 물을 준 꽃이니까요.

You are beautiful, but you are empty. One could not die for you. To be sure, an ordinary passerby would think that my rose lookes just like you — the rose that belongs to me. But in herself alone she is more important than all the hundreds of you other roses; because it is she that I have watered.

You are beautiful, but you are empty. One could not die for you. To be sure, an ordinary passerby would think that my rose lookes just like you — the rose that belongs to me. But in herself alone she is more important than all the hundreds of you other roses; because it is she that I have watered.

- '어린 왕자' 중에서 -

You are beautiful, but you are empty. One could not die for you. To be sure, an ordinary passerby would think that my rose looks just like you the rose that belongs to me. But in herself alone she is more important than all the hundreds of you other roses; because it is she that I have watered.

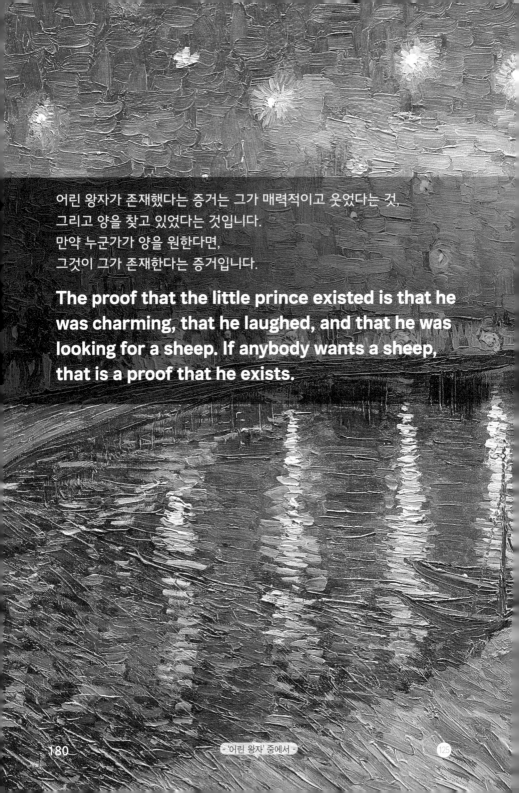

어린 왕자가 존재했다는 증거는 그가 매력적이고 웃었다는 것,
그리고 양을 찾고 있었다는 것입니다.
만약 누군가가 양을 원한다면,
그것이 그가 존재한다는 증거입니다.

**The proof that the little prince existed is that he
was charming, that he laughed, and that he was
looking for a sheep. If anybody wants a sheep,
that is a proof that he exists.**

- '어린 왕자' 중에서 -

The proof that the little prince existed is
that he was charming, that he laughed, and
that he was looking for a sheep. If anybody
wants a sheep, that is a proof that he exists.

The proof that the little prince existed is
that he was charming, that he laughed, and
that he was looking for a sheep. If anybody
wants a sheep, that is a proof that he exists.

하루 한 그림

오늘은 어반스케치

펜 드로잉부터 수채화까지

김미경 지음 | 17,000원

하루 한 그림

오늘은 오일파스텔

오롯이 나를 위한 조용한 시간!

김지은 지음 | 15,000원

하루 한 그림

오늘은 캔버스 위의 아크릴화

멋진 화가가 된 듯한 느낌

김지은 지음 | 14,000원

오늘은 색연필 컬러링북

화투

김정희 지음 | 14,000원

오늘은 색연필 컬러링북

라온민화 꿈해몽

이다감 지음 | 14,000원

오늘은 색연필 컬러링북

라온민화

이다감 지음 | 14,000원

치매예방을 위한
오늘도 재밌는 뇌운동 1
숨은그림찾기: 연중행사 편
큰그림 편집부 | 8,500원

치매예방을 위한
오늘도 재밌는 뇌운동 2 (스티커240)
숨은그림찾기: 전래동화 편
큰그림 편집부 | 10,000원

치매예방을 위한
오늘도 재밌는 뇌운동 3 (스티커270)
숨은그림찾기: 추억놀이 편
큰그림 편집부 | 10,000원

다짜고짜 수성펜
쉽게 따라 그리는 수성펜 풍경화
김정희 지음 | 13,000원

예쁜 손글씨에
아름다운 시를 더하다
윤동주, 김소월, 정지용 외 저 | 8,500원

한자를 알면 어휘가 보인다
김정희 외 4인의 한시 24수
김정희, 이황, 김시습 외 | 8,500원

챗GPT가 골라주는 **영어명언**¹²⁵

: 필기체로 따라쓰기 :

초판 발행   2024년 12월 15일

지은이   큰그림 편집부
펴낸이   이강실
펴낸곳   도서출판 큰그림
등 록   제2018-000090호
주 소   서울시 마포구 양화로 133 서교타워 1703호
전 화   02-849-5069
팩 스   02-6004-5970
이메일   big_picture_41@naver.com

기   획   이강실
교정교열   김선미
디 자 인   예다움
인쇄와 제본   미래피앤피

가 격   12,000원
ISBN   979-11-90976-32-9 (13740)